LEARN.
ADVENTURES!

Summer

Publisher ....*Arthur L. Miley*

Editor ....*Crystal Abell*

Art Director ....*Debbie Birch*

Illustrators ....*Fran Kizer*

Roger Johnson

Unless otherwise indicated, all Scripture is taken from the KING JAMES VERSION of the Bible.
Scripture marked (NIV) is taken from the HOLY BIBLE, NEW INTERNATIONAL VERSION.
Copyright © 1973, 1978, 1984 International Bible Society.
Used by permission of Zondervan Bible Publishers.

Portions of the *Learning Adventures* series were previously published
as part of the *Creative Church Parties* series.
Copyright © 1991 Rainbow Publishers.

Copyright 1997 • Second Printing
Rainbow Books • P.O. Box 261129 • San Diego, CA 92196

#RB36314
ISBN 1-885358-14-8

TABLE OF CONTENTS

INTRODUCTION

Welcome to a great time of fun and learning about God–*Learning Adventures!* The purpose of these group functions is to teach young children about the Bible. Each activity is an excellent teaching tool that complements your current classroom instruction in a fun way that involves the kids. While these action programs provide for creative play, their ultimate purpose is to reinforce lessons from the Bible.

This book is very teacher-friendly! Each book in the *Learning Adventures* series contains eighteen age-appropriate activities that will help you teach biblical concepts in a fun, adventurous way. Each activity contains the following:

- **Lesson Idea** that explains the biblical concepts that are the focus of the activity.
- **Memory Verse** to reinforce the lesson.
- **Multiple Activity Suggestions** that can be used all at once or spread out over a number of meetings to make each day special.
- **Devotions** that will help the Bible come alive for young children. These devotions are also age-appropriate and thus may be read directly to the children.
- **Reproducible Invitation** and publicity suggestions to maximize participation of the kids.
- **Decoration and Preparation instructions** that will help you easily create a fun, exciting environment for the kids.
- **Refreshment suggestions**.

These activities require only simple planning and preparation–you determine how elaborate they will be. Our hope is that this book will help you create an exciting learning environment that will reinforce biblical lessons. Have fun teaching the children about God's Word!

Ages 2 & 3

Summer Sleepy-Time

Memory Verse: "I am with you always." Matthew 28:20

 **IDEA** The fun of coming "dressed up" in their pajamas with stuffed animals and dolls in tow will make this get-together a special one for your students. The children will learn that God is always with us, even when we are sleeping.

PUBLICITY

Write the date, time, and place on the invitation pattern and duplicate.

For other publicity, write the information on small pieces of paper and pin or tape them to a pillow. Set the pillow in a location where the parents are sure to see it.

Be sure to remind the parents to dress their children in comfortable pajamas; you will need to clarify that the children will *not* be spending the night. The boys and girls should also bring their own pillows and favorite stuffed animals or dolls.

DECORATIONS & PREPARATION

Make the room look like a sleepy-time haven by duplicating the star and moon patterns and hanging the cut stars and moons from the ceiling. If you wish, make the stars shiny by covering with aluminum foil.

Duplicate and cut out more stars to place in various spots around the room for a later activity.

ACTIVITIES

Sleepy Star Search

What you'll need: Duplicated stars and small paper bags

"Hide" the stars around the room ahead of time (see Preparation). Give each child a paper bag and allow the children time to get as many stars as they can find.

Bedtime Story

What you'll need: Story book with cassette tape and a tape player, picture books for the children

Many storybooks now come with narration and sound effects provided on a cassette tape. Find an appropriate book for your class, perhaps one with a bedtime theme. If your church does not have books such as these available, you might try your local library or a bookstore.

Provide picture books for the children to "read" themselves when the story is finished.

Sleepy-Time Song

To the tune of "Here We Go 'Round The Mulberry Bush," teach the children the following sing-along song with appropriate actions:

This is the way we brush our teeth,
　　Brush our teeth, brush our teeth.
This is the way we brush our teeth
　　Before we go to bed.

Other verses:
This is the way we wash our face.
This is the way we say a prayer.

Now I Lay Me Down to Sleep

Introduce the toddlers to the traditional rhyming prayer. Ask the children to fold their hands and repeat these words after you:

Now I lay me down to sleep;
　　I pray the Lord my soul to keep.
Please keep me safe throughout the night,
　　And wake me with the morning light.
Amen.

REFRESHMENTS

Let each child help make his own cup of hot chocolate to drink. Provide ready-made cocoa mix for the children to spoon into cups; pour in heated water (not too hot!) and let the children stir. Serve with homemade cookies.

DEVOTIONS

The account of Jesus walking on the water can help your students see that He is always with us. Open your Bible to Matthew 14:22-33 so the children will associate the story with the Bible:

It had been a long day. Jesus was very tired and wanted to be alone to pray, so His friends got into a boat to go to the other side of the lake.

The wind was blowing very hard. Jesus saw His friends and started walking on the water toward them. They didn't know who it was and were afraid, but Jesus said, "Don't be afraid."

Peter wanted to be sure it was really Jesus coming toward the boat. He said he wanted to walk on the water, too. He stepped out of the boat and started walking on the water, but then he took his eyes off Jesus. He became afraid and started to sink. What do you think happened to Peter? Jesus pulled him up and they got into the boat together. Everyone knew this was truly Jesus.

Ask the children if they sometimes get scared in the dark. What can they do when they are afraid? Is Jesus with us all the time, even when we are asleep?

Say, **In Matthew 28:20, Jesus says, "I am with you always." He is constantly watching over us, even when we are tucked away in bed.**

Repeat the Bible verse several times with the children. Close in a brief prayer, thanking God that He is with us.

INVITATION

It's a Summer Sleepy-Time!

☆ come dressed in pajamas and bring your favorite stuffed animal or doll!

DATE

TIME

PLACE

PATTERNS FOR DUPLICATION

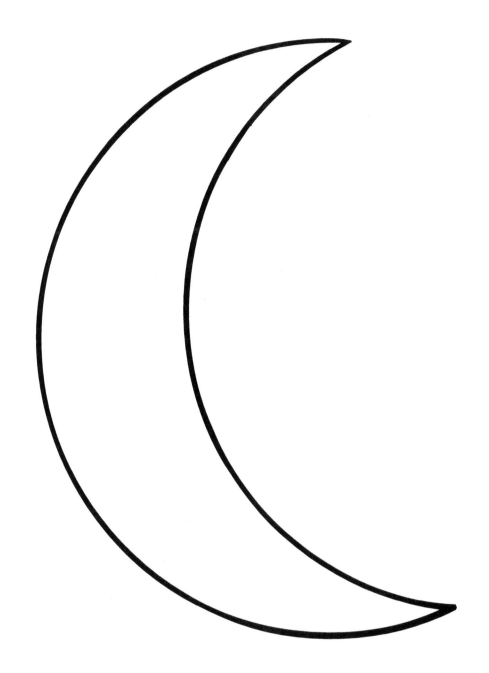

Here We Go A-Boating

Memory Verse: "Even the wind and the waves obey Him."
Mark 4:41 (NIV)

IDEA
This plan offers an opportunity for the children to have some fun with boats of all kinds, even in the refreshments. Many stories about Jesus involve a boat, as your students will learn in a lesson about Jesus' power over the sea.

PUBLICITY
Fill in the necessary details on the invitation pattern and duplicate enough for your expected guests.

Enlarge the pattern for a poster. To make it extra noticeable, tape the poster to a toy boat placed in a large bowl of water.

DECORATIONS & PREPARATION
Cut out pictures of boats from magazines and place them around the room.

Make a fun sitting area for some of the activities and the devotions by setting up a make-believe boat. Make it out of cardboard boxes, chairs, blankets or whatever you wish.

ACTIVITIES
Sand Boat Picture
What you'll need: Powdered paint, fine sand, a boat pattern, blank paper, drawing paper, pencils, squeeze-bottle glue, large spoons, and paint shirts

Ahead of time, mix about 1-2 Tbsp. powdered paint to every cup of fine sand to get the desired shade. Use the boat on the invitation pattern as a guide or find a picture of a boat to trace onto a sheet of paper for each child.

Due to its potential to be messy, this activity might best be held outdoors. You will need extra helpers so that each child can be helped to complete this activity. Each child should have a paint shirt to protect his clothing. (Small men's shirts may be worn backwards.) Hold the glue bottle with the child to squeeze out the glue around the boat shape and within the boat to make a fun design.

Have each child scoop out some of the colored sand with a large spoon and then pour it over the glue. Help him shake off the excess sand. Set the picture aside to allow the glue to dry. Explain that the sand will adhere to the glue to make an interesting boat picture.

Playdough Boat
What you'll need: Flour, salt, salad oil, water, food coloring, and mixing bowl

Mix together 3 cups flour, 1 cup salt, and 1½ tsp. salad oil, adding water until you get the right consistency for dough. Add food coloring to make different colors.

Help the children make a boat with the dough. Ask, **If you could ride in this boat, where would you want to go?** Let the boys and girls continue playing until you are ready to begin the next activity.

Row, Row, Row Your Boat
What you'll need: Room to play

Have children sit in pairs facing each other. Ask them to hold hands and together sing "Row, Row, Row Your Boat." Sing it a few times and make up additional verses such as "Fish, fish, fish we'll catch" and "Fun, fun, fun we'll have."

REFRESHMENTS
For a fun snack, your students will make "Berry-Banana Boats." Slice bananas in half crosswise and then lengthwise. Give two quarter pieces of banana to each child to make a "banana boat" in his bowl. Place a scoop of ice cream or frozen yogurt

on each boat. Let the child add a few spoonfuls of berries to the ice cream.

If the children so desire, you may put a touch of whipping cream on top of the berries and one more berry on top of the whipping cream. Serve with cold water.

DEVOTIONS

Many Bible stories relate in some way to boats. To help your students see that God calls us to obey Him, share the story of how Jesus commanded the wind and the waves to obey Him.

Let the children get into their make-believe boat. Open your Bible to Mark 4:35-41 so the boys and girls associate the story with the Bible. Encourage them to "follow the leader," acting out parts of the story with you:

Jesus and His friends were very tired after a long day (rub eyes and yawn). **They decided to get into a boat to cross the lake.**

The boat began to rock (rock back and forth). **Suddenly the wind blew harder and the waves crashed against the boat** (rock harder in the boat and make "swoosh" sounds). **Everyone was afraid, except for Jesus. Jesus was asleep in the boat** (fold hands underneath head like a pillow).

Jesus' friends woke Him up and said, "Look, we are going to drown." Jesus said, "Why are you afraid?" Jesus put out His hand and said, "Peace! Be still!" The wind stopped and the waves stopped (stop rocking motion and swoosh sound).

Jesus' friends were amazed and said, "Even the wind and the waves obey Him." That's our special Bible verse for today. It is found in the book of Mark. Let's say it together.

Share with the boys and girls that Jesus wants us to obey Him, too. We need to listen to what Jesus says. Repeat the verse, then close with a brief prayer asking God to help us obey.

INVITATION

FIRST CLASS SAILOR

Student's Name

"Even the wind and the waves obey Him!"
Mark 4:41

Group Leader's Name

Date

Super Senses

Memory Verse: "Believe on the Lord Jesus Christ." Acts 16:31

IDEA Your students are just discovering what their five senses are and how to use them. These activities will help the children have fun exploring the senses and teach them about a woman who was healed by a special touch.

PUBLICITY

Fill in the details on the invitation pattern and duplicate for all the children. Enlarge the invitation to make a poster, decorating it with magazine pictures of children's faces and hands.

DECORATIONS & PREPARATION

Decorate the room with things that are appropriate to develop the theme of the five senses: different types of fabric to emphasize touch, a few bells for sound, perhaps some simmering potpourri for smell, a variety of fruit to emphasize taste, and colorful pictures for sight.

You will need to make a tape recording of various sounds familiar to the children. Some ideas include: running water, an opening and closing door, a doorbell, a piano, a washing machine, a telephone, a blender, a pencil sharpener, a mixer, a vacuum cleaner, and a clock. Include a short pause between each sound.

ACTIVITIES

What's Missing?
What you'll need: Variety of fruit, toys, and plastic animals (some the same, some different), and a tray

Put three different objects on the tray. Ask the children to close their eyes while you take one object away. Let the children guess what is missing. Repeat this action several times.

Next put three objects on the tray—two being the same and one different. Ask which one is differ-ent and why. If the children are good at identifying three objects you may add a fourth and continue to increase by one in each succeeding round of play.

What Sound Is It?
What you'll need: Tape recording of familiar sounds (see Preparation) and a cassette player

Play the tape while the children are sitting quietly in a circle. Stop after each sound and let the boys and girls guess what it is.

Sense Explorers
What you'll need: Safe walking area and small paper bags

Take a short walk and focus the children's interest on their different senses. Using the sense of sight, help the children to focus on the beautiful colors. Using the sense of hearing, focus on the variety of sounds. Using the sense of smell, let the children appreciate the scent of flowers and freshly cut grass. Using the sense of touch, allow the children to pick up a variety of objects, such as rocks, leaves, wild flowers, and twigs, and place these in a small paper bag.

A Touch of Nature
What you'll need: Paper bag with nature objects from last activity

Let the children take one object at a time out of their nature bags. Compare the touch of each object. Another way to do this is to call out individual items and compare their textures. For example, contrast all the rocks at the same time, and so on.

REFRESHMENTS

Put a scoop of frozen yogurt in a cone for each child. Let the boys and girls choose from a selection of toppings, such as crushed peanuts, granola, chocolate chips, broken cookies, etc. Keep wet washcloths on hand for messy fingers.

DEVOTIONS

The faith of one woman in the Bible relied upon merely touching the hem of Jesus' garment, and the woman was healed. Turn to Mark 5:21-34 or Luke 8:40-48 so the children will associate this story with the Bible:

Many people were crowding around Jesus one day. The people pushed one way and then the other way so they could get close to Jesus.

One woman had been sick for many years. She had gone to many doctors, but no one could make her better. The woman thought, *If only I could get close to Jesus, He would make me well.*

Finally, she got close enough to touch His robe, and she was healed! Jesus felt someone touch Him and asked who it was. When the woman said, "I touched you," Jesus told her, "You are well now, because you believed in Me."

Share the special Bible verse, Acts 16:31, with the children: "Believe on the Lord Jesus Christ." Say, **We believe in Jesus because He is God's Son. He can do special things that no one else can do.**

Repeat the verse several times. End the devotional with prayer, thanking God for the senses He gives us and for helping us to believe in His Son.

INVITATION

PLEASE COME AND BRING YOUR

SUPER SENSES

DATE   TIME   PLACE

GOD GIVES US OUR SENSES!

Student's Name

I used all five senses at the Super Senses Group!

Church Name

Date

Group Leader's Name

Creative Campout

Memory Verse: "The Lord is my Helper." Hebrews 13:6

IDEA Camping means being outdoors and having fun with friends. This get-together will give the children an opportunity to learn how God took care of the Israelites while they camped in the desert for forty years and how much God cares for us, too.

PUBLICITY

Add the details to the invitation pattern and duplicate one for each guest expected.

Enlarge the pattern to make a poster. Decorate with scraps of fabric glued onto the tent and a variety of stars and stickers.

DECORATIONS & PREPARATION

In moderation, set up camping equipment throughout the room. If you do not have access to a tent, throw a blanket over some chairs instead.

Use a cooler to store the food items for refreshment time. You will need a barbecue.

ACTIVITIES

A Camping We Will Go

Sing "A-Camping We Will Go" to the tune of "The Farmer in The Dell" with the children. Add as many extra verses as you like, such as "A tent we will bring," "Delicious food we'll eat," and so forth.

Baggy Backpacks

What you'll need: Paper bags, crayons, stickers, strips of fabric, stapler, and tape

Give each child a paper bag, double strength, to color and decorate with stickers to make a backpack. Make sure to write the children's names on the bags.

Staple two strips of fabric to one side to make loopholes for the arms. Cover the staples with tape for safety. The children may use these "backpacks" to load up their "gear."

Orange Refresher

What you'll need: Blender, nonfat plain yogurt, water, frozen orange juice, honey, vanilla, ice cubes, and an airtight container

Let the children help you pour the following ingredients into a blender: 1 cup nonfat plain yogurt, 1 cup water, 6 oz. can frozen orange juice (unsweetened), 1/3 cup honey, 1 tsp. vanilla, and 8-10 ice cubes. Blend until smooth and pour into an airtight container for the camping trip.

Packing Up

What you'll need: Backpacks from earlier activity, play clothes, and play kitchen equipment

Packing up for the camping trip can be fun. Discuss with the children what kinds of things they should bring on their camping trip. Provide various items at learning centers around the room, such as a housekeeping center where the young students can choose plates, cups, bowls, cutlery, and so on. Let the guests go around the room and collect whatever they wish, putting the "gear" into their backpacks.

REFRESHMENTS

If you have enough adult help available, barbecue some hamburgers and hot dogs. Set out a variety of condiments for the children to choose from. Serve with potato chips and carrot sticks, and remember to pour cups of the orange drink made earlier.

DEVOTIONS

What you'll need: Corn Flakes cereal.

For 40 years the children of Israel wandered in the desert, constantly putting up their tents in new places. In all that time, God always took care of His people. Open your Bible to Exodus 16 so the children associate the story with the Bible:

The people of Israel lived in their tents for many years. During the day they would walk a long way and at nighttime they would put up their tents. This was a time when they needed to trust God because they didn't know if they would have food when they got hungry or water when they got thirsty. Their leader Moses told them not to worry. God would provide food for everyone to eat.

At breakfast, God would send manna. It tasted something like this (give each child a handful of corn flakes cereal). **At dinner time, the people could catch birds called quail. God provided water for the people, too.**

God took good care of the Israelites. He takes good care of us, too. Can you think of some ways that God takes care of us?

Our verse for today is Hebrews 13:6, "The Lord is my Helper." Let's say it several times.

Invite a child to thank God for being our Helper and always taking care of us.

INVITATION

I HAD FUN WITH MY FRIENDS

at the

CREATIVE CAMPOUT

Student's Name

Group Leader's Name

Date

Ages 4 & 5

Farm Fest

Memory Verse: "(God) makes grass grow for the cattle, and plants for man. . . (to bring) forth food from the earth." Psalm 104:14 (NIV)

IDEA

The fun of exploring the wonders of a farm is sure to delight your students, but even if you cannot locate a real barnyard, the animal games will provide plenty of fun. The children will also be able to appreciate how we use our God-given resources.

PUBLICITY

If you can borrow a toy farm from a student's family or the church nursery, set it up in your meeting room for a few weeks. Enlarge the barn pattern (after filling in the details) to make a poster for displaying next to the farm set.

Duplicate the pattern at regular size to make invitations.

DECORATIONS & PREPARATION

Schedule the Farm Fest well in advance in order to have time to find a suitable location. The ideal location for this party is, of course, a farm or ranch. Ask people in your congregation for suggestions, or perhaps a church of your denomination in a rural area can help you locate an appropriate spot.

If you can't find a farm or even a rural home, try to find an open field, large playground, park, or other area where there is plenty of space and you can rope off an area for a "corral." Try to secure a couple of bales of hay or a pile of dry grass to add atmosphere and use in the games.

When the site has been decided on you may want to survey it ahead of time and decide what can be done. Explain to the property owners what you plan to do—that part of the purpose of the event is to be educational—and that you would like for them to give a short tour for the children. Get permission for all other activities.

If the location is far from your church be sure to make plans for transportation by bus or ask some parents to drive.

Duplicate the animal patterns to make name tags for the children. Have a pen and some safety pins ready at the meeting place so you can give out the name tags as the children arrive.

ACTIVITIES

The structure of the event will largely depend on the location, so make adjustments as necessary.

Explore the Farm

If you've found a large farm for the fest, begin with the tour. Introduce the property owner to the children and let him lead the group to see the animals, equipment, and maybe some of the work that is going on. He could also explain at that time any off-limits areas. Since it is ssummer there may be baby animals to watch.

Noisy Farm

Divide the group into four teams, only instead of numbering off one to four, use four animal names. For instance, tell Kenny he is a cow, Chrissy is a duck, Jamie is a sheep, Karen is a piglet, then back to cow, and so on. When you give the signal, each child is to begin making the sound of his animal and try to find the others who are making the same sound. (You might need to tell them what sounds to make.) When the noise finally ends you'll have four teams. Combine them to make just two teams for the games.

Feed the Pigs

What you'll need: Pig trough or other receptacle and six corn cobs

Line up two relay teams several feet from an

empty pig trough, water trough, large pans, or other containers. Ask a couple of helpers to stand behind the trough facing the teams.

Give the first player on each team three corn cobs (bean bags will work as substitutes). At the starting signal, the players will throw their cobs one at a time into the trough. The helpers will bring the cobs back to the next children in line and also keep score of cobs thrown in the trough.

Hay Bale Tag
What you'll need: Hay

Use a bale of hay as the base and allow only one person at a time to be safe on the base. Whenever "It" touches someone who isn't touching the hay, that child becomes the new "It."

Jumping Jacks and Jills
What you'll need: Two pieces of rope and prizes

Tape one length of rope to the floor and place the second rope close to the first, but do not tape it. This will be the "chicken jump," which everyone should be able to make. After everyone has had a turn, move the rope out a little for the "bunny hop." Move it further for the "goat leap." Next will be the "steer stomp" and then the "horse hurdle." Give a small prize, such as an animal eraser or something similar, to any who can make the horse hurdle.

REFRESHMENTS

Tell the children ahead of time to bring sack lunches and provide punch or lemonade. Also provide food that comes from the farmer's crops. For example, if he grows wheat, you could bring a loaf of wheat bread.

DEVOTIONS

If you are within view of a field, tell the children to look in that direction. As the farmer will probably be in the middle of the growing season, talk about how the little seeds that he plants grow into big healthy plants. Those plants are where we get our food like corn on the cob or beans, etc.

Ask, **Where did those seeds come from?** Read Genesis 1:11 and then tell students, **God created the world, He made the seeds. God made all the trees and the plants. He made everything.**

Invite your host to lead the children in saying the memory verse. Ask him to offer a prayer of thanksgiving for the Lord's creation.

INVITATION PATTERN

PATTERNS FOR DUPLICATION

Name _____

Name _____

Name _____

Name _____

Buddy Day

Memory Verse: "Dear friends, let us love one another, for love comes from God." I John 4:7 (NIV)

IDEA

Your preschoolers are learning what it means to have friends. A "Buddy Day" is a fun way to teach about friendship and sharing. Encourage your students to bring a friend with them to the event.

PUBLICITY

Fill in the details on the invitation and duplicate. To make a poster, enlarge the pattern and then animate it with a picture of people holding hands or talking or sharing (cut out from a magazine or leftover teaching resources).

DECORATIONS & PREPARATION

Use more pictures, such as the one used for the poster, to hang around the room. Secure them to the walls and/or hang with string from the ceiling.

ACTIVITIES

Find Your Buddy

What you'll need: Duplicated sheet of animals

Duplicate the sheet twice so that there are two cards for each animal (or, if your group is larger, make three copies). Give each child a card, making sure each one has a match. (For instance, if you give out a pig card to one student, give out another pig card to someone else.)

Instruct the children to find their animal-buddies by making the noises of the animals on their cards: the children having duck cards will look for each other by saying, "Quack, quack," and so on. If you have an odd number of students, give yourself a card as well so that no children are left out. When all animal-buddy teams are located, have the children turn in their cards. If you wish, the cards can be distributed to different children, and the animal-buddies can try to locate each other again.

Stick with Your Buddy Relay

What you'll need: Room to play

Group the children into two lines. The buddies from the last game should stay together. The first two buddies in each line will face each other, cross arms, and hold hands. When you give the signal, they will hurry to a set goal across the room and back to the end of the line. The next buddies will do the same, and so on, until all have run. The team who finishes the relay first may be given a small prize.

Ball Buddies

What you'll need: One ball for every pair of children

If you wish, play Find Your Buddy again to get a new group of pairs for this game. Have the pairs stand five feet apart from each other. Give buddies a ball to toss back and forth. After a minute or so, tell the children to all take a step backwards and resume tossing the ball. Continue having the pairs get farther apart until they tire of the game or it is too much of a challenge.

REFRESHMENTS

Serve ice cream sundaes and emphasize sharing at the same time. Allow the children to choose from a variety of toppings, but have them go to the tables in pairs so that one child will scoop a topping for another. You can have chocolate, marshmallow, butterscotch, etc., along with whipped cream, nuts, and cherries. Have cold water available to drink.

DEVOTIONS

Open your Bible to I Samuel 18:1-4 and tell the story of the friendship between Jonathan and David. Ask the children, **How did Jonathan show his friendship to David?** (He loved him and he shared things with him.)

Invite the children to tell the names of some of their friends—they may be from the church or perhaps from their neighborhoods. Encourage them to share what they like about their friends.

Tell the children that we have another Friend who likes to share with us, too. That Friend is Jesus. He understands when we are sad, and He is happy when we feel happy, too. He loves us very much.

Repeat the memory verse, then pray with the children, thanking Jesus that He is always our Friend.

INVITATION PATTERN

BRING YOUR PAL, BRING YOUR FRIEND, WE'LL LAUGH AND PLAY UNTIL THE END OF

BUDDY DAY

DATE: TIME:

PLACE:

OINK!

MOO!
MOO!

BOW-
WOW!

CHEEP!
CHEEP!

MEOW!

NEIGH!

BAA!
BAA!

QUACK!
QUACK!

EE-EE-EE

GRR!

ROAR!

HOOT!
HOOT!

GOD GIVES US FRIENDS!

Student's Name

&

Student's Name

We're Buddies!

Church Name

Group Leader's Name

Date

Zany Zoo

Memory Verse: "Blessed be the Lord, Who daily loadeth us with benefits." Psalm 68:19

IDEA

What child can resist the wonders and excitement of the animals at the zoo? This get-together will offer fun with a familiar subject as well as help the children see that God takes good care of us.

PUBLICITY

Fill in the details on the invitation and duplicate. Enlarge the pattern to make a poster. If desired, color in the animals to brighten things up, or cut out pictures of actual animals from magazines and paste on.

For an added touch, place stuffed animals borrowed from the children or the nursery in a conspicuous spot and display the poster with them.

DECORATIONS & PREPARATION

Use the stuffed animals borrowed for the publicity as part of your decorations, and/or cut out more pictures from magazines.

Another idea would be to find coloring books with animals in them for the children to color as they arrive. You could hang these around the room during the meeting and then let the children take them home.

To make the get-together more interesting, try to invite someone representing the local zoo to come for 15 minutes or so. This person could talk about what he does at the zoo and maybe even bring in an animal for the children to touch and feel.

ACTIVITIES

Lions, Bears, and Sheep
What you'll need: Circle of chairs

Count the number of children present and subtract one. Arrange this number of chairs in a circle to play this variation of "Fruit Basket Upset."

Select one child to be "It." Whisper in the ear of each remaining student one of these words: *lion, bear,* or *sheep.* Then say aloud, "Lions and bears change places." All of those named *lion* and *bear* should hurry to exchange places before "It" gets one of the empty chairs. The child left without a place becomes the new "It."

Monkey Cage
What you'll need: Room to play

Select a child to be "It" and have groups of two or three hold hands to form a "cage." All the other players are "monkeys" and must stand in a cage. When you give the signal, the monkeys must change cages. "It" then tries to get in a cage. Monkeys without cages then become "Its."

Duck Walk
What you'll need: Room to play

Line the children up against a wall or starting line. Show them how to squat and grasp their ankles with their hands. They are to try to "waddle" as far as they can toward the other end of the room. Have a contest to see who can waddle the farthest before tipping over or letting go of his ankles. Select children for first, second, and third places, if you wish. Award small prizes.

A Visitor from the Zoo

If you were able to line up someone to come from the zoo, give him the floor for a while. Make sure the children have specific instructions about whether they may touch any animals he may have brought along, and if they may, how to do so. They will probably have a load of questions for your guest to answer.

REFRESHMENTS

Take the children to wash their hands, especially after handling animals. Let the children snack on gummy bears and animal crackers before you bring out an animal cake. Cut two round layers to form a lion, bear, elephant, or any other kind of animal and use various sizes, shapes, and colors of candy to decorate. Serve with fruit punch.

DEVOTIONS

Ask the children what it might be like to be in a zoo. Whatever their answers, try to emphasize that the zoo keepers take good care of the animals, giving them food and water, helping them when they are sick, and giving them a nice place to live where they can see other animals, too.

Say to the children that we do not live in the zoo, but there is someone who takes care of us all the time. Do they know who that person is? Read Isaiah 41:10, 17-18 to "give" the answer. Ask the students, **Are there times when you are afraid? These verses tell us that God is with us. Even though we cannot see God, He is always watching over us from heaven. He takes good care of us. Whatever we need, He is able to help us. And He does this because He loves us.**

Say the memory verse with the boys and girls. Close with prayer, thanking God that He cares about us enough to take care of us like no one else can.

INVITATION PATTERN

America's Birthday Bash

Memory Verse: "Refuse the evil, and choose the good."
Isaiah 7:15

IDEA
Most children of preschool age know that we celebrate birthdays with parties, so use this idea to observe the Fourth of July. On this holiday we sing the praises of our democratic freedoms; the children in your class can discover that God gives us freedom as well: the freedom to choose between right and wrong.

PUBLICITY
Include the date, time, and location on the invitation pattern and duplicate. Decorate with red and blue stars. To make a poster, enlarge the pattern; decorate by gluing on confetti made out of red and blue pieces of construction paper and a hole punch.

DECORATIONS & PREPARATION
Use red, white, and blue crepe paper to decorate the room and the refreshment table; use a medium-sized United States flag on a staff as a centerpiece.

Buy red, white, and blue candy, miniature flags, or other Fourth of July souvenirs for game prizes.

You will need long tables for several of the activities, so make sure these are set up ahead of time.

ACTIVITIES

Fireworks Finger Painting
What you'll need: Finger Paints, black construction paper, newspaper, and paint shirts

Set up the newspaper to protect the area from "accidents" and give each child a paint shirt for the same purpose. Let the students use the finger paints for five minutes or so; for this craft it would be better for them to make blotches rather than particular drawings. Tell them to use the paint toward the center of the paper rather than the edges.

When the boys and girls are done painting, help them make "fireworks" by folding the paper in half lengthwise and smoothing it out so that the paint goes in several directions. When the paper is unfolded, the paint will look like a spray of colorful fireworks.

Set the papers aside to dry, making sure the children's names are on them first.

Thirteen Colonies
What you'll need: Enlarged and duplicated map of thirteen colonies, and an eraser

Enlarge and duplicate the sheet designated for this game and color it in if you wish. Place the map on the floor or on a table and line up the students a few feet away from the map. The children will have three turns to throw an eraser to land on one of the 13 colonies, earning points corresponding to the number on the colony. Keep track of the points so you can award prizes to the top three.

Hold the Fort
What you'll need: Long tables and ping pong balls

Have the children kneel around all four sides of one or two long tables, depending on the size of the group. One side of each table and one half of each end will constitute one army; the other side and other half of each end will be the opposing army.

Tell the children to keep their hands behind their backs. Give a ping pong ball to one army at each table to begin the game. The object of the game is for that army to "hold the fort" by blowing the ping pong ball across the table, through the enemy's line, and off onto the floor. The opposing army tries to prevent the attack by blowing the ball back and off the table on its opponent's side. Award the winning team with small prizes.

REFRESHMENTS

What would a birthday be without cake and ice cream? Make the cake decorations in keeping with the theme and serve with generous scoops of vanilla ice cream. Provide ice water or red punch to drink. Remember to sing "Happy Birthday" to America before you dig in!

DEVOTIONS

Ask the children if they have had fun celebrating America's birthday. Tell them that the United States became a country a long time ago, before they were born, and people have been giving America a birthday celebration every year since.

Say, **One of the reasons the United States became a country was so that we could make special choices for ourselves. That is what it means to be free, or to have freedom.**

Read II Corinthians 3:17 and tell the children that God helps us to be free, too. He wants us to be able to make the right choices. Repeat the memory verse with the students, then ask, **What do you think are some of the happy choices that God wants us to make?** (To listen to mommy, to help sister pick up the toys, to be nice to my friends, etc.)

Pray with the boys and girls that they would let God help them to be free and make the choices that will please Him.

INVITATION PATTERN

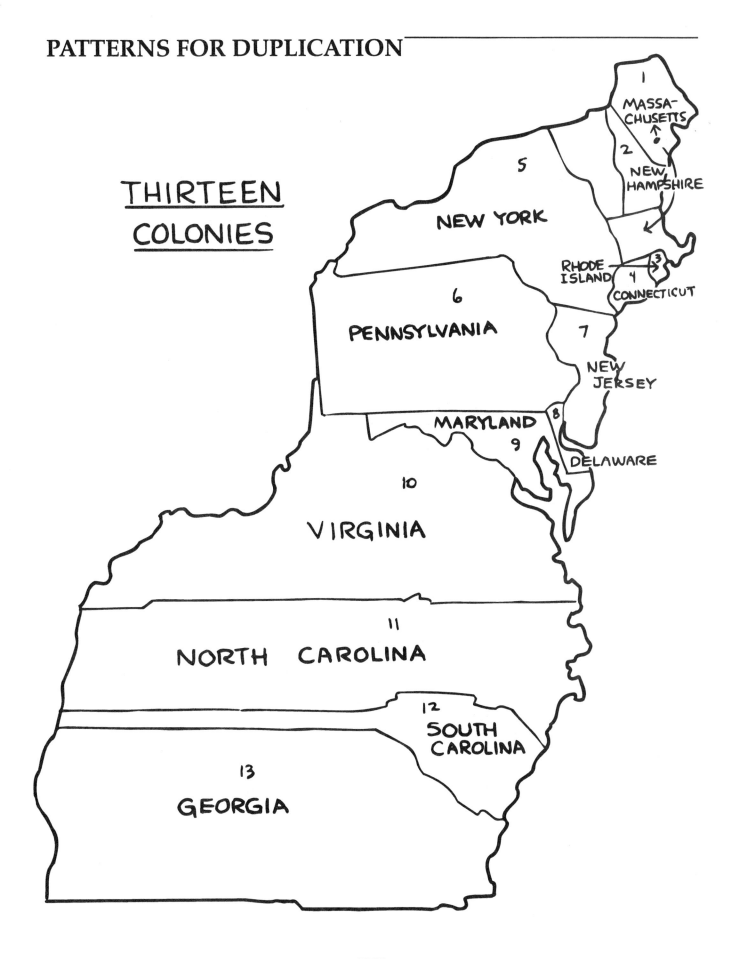

THIRTEEN
COLONIES

Little Olympics

Memory Verse: "I press on toward the goal to win the prize for which God has called me. . ."
Philippians 3:14 (NIV)

IDEA The Olympic Games are noted not only for the great athletic events, but also because of the level of participation from so many countries. This get-together allows your students the opportunity for some outdoor fun and a chance to see that God believes we are all winners.

PUBLICITY

Write the date, time, and place of the event on the invitation pattern and duplicate. For making a poster, enlarge the pattern and then cut out "doughnuts" from blue, black, red, yellow, and green construction paper. Place these over the rings on the pattern in the following order from left to right: top three—blue, black, and red; bottom two—yellow and green. Cut a slit in each circle so that you can overlap the rings together.

DECORATIONS & PREPARATION

If at all possible you will want to hold this event outdoors at a park or recreation center, so decorations will not be necessary.

Part of the focus of the event will be that every one of us is a winner in God's sight. To help emphasize this, let every child "win" at the games by awarding medals. This way the children will all have something when the get-together is over.

Duplicate the medal pattern several times onto gold construction paper to award those who actually win the games, and duplicate onto another color (or a variety of colors) for the "regular" medals. Tie a loop of yarn through the holes so that the medals can hang around the children's necks.

ACTIVITIES

Baton Relay
What you'll need: Lounge chair and paper towel or wrapping paper tubes
Group the children into teams of four and have them stand behind a starting line. Set up a lounge chair or other object about twenty five feet away. Give the first child on each team a cardboard tube "baton" and instruct him to run toward the chair, circle around it, then run back and give the baton to the next child on his team. For variety have the children actually sit in the chair before coming back to the line. Award gold medals to the winning team and regular medals to the rest of the children.

Terrific Tumbling
What you'll need: Blankets
All of your students should be able to perform some sort of tumbling activity for this "event." For instance, several will be able to do somersaults, a few might know how to do a cartwheel, and probably everyone will be able to do a simple pirouette.

Place several blankets on top of each other to provide a makeshift tumbling mat. Give each child a chance to show the others what he can do. If you wish, offer gold medals to those who can do the most or the fastest, etc., or you may simply want to award a gold medal to every child, no matter what he does.

Super Jump
What you'll need: Masking tape
Line up the children with their toes on a marked starting line. At the signal, all jump forward five times. This can be done for fun at first, then do it as a contest. Use pieces of masking tape to mark the distances. Give a gold medal to the top three jumpers and a regular medal to the rest.

REFRESHMENTS

It would be fun to serve up an "international" lunch of frankfurters (Germany), potato salad (Ireland), tortilla chips (Mexico), and tropical fruit punch (Caribbean). Serve a sheet cake decorated with the Olympic rings.

DEVOTIONS

Read the medals. Say, "God believes we are winners because He loves us. We can pretend that life is a race, and that we are trying to win a medal or a prize. In I Corinthians 9:25 (read this) we see that the prize, or crown, that we are trying to win will last forever. Ask, What could that prize be? Will it be a medal like the ones you got today? No, it is much better than that.

Read II Timothy 4:7-8 and say, Our prize for making the right choices and living the way God wants us to is to live in heaven with Him forever.

Repeat the memory verse with the boys and girls and close with prayer, asking God to help the children make those right choices and to "win the prize."

INVITATION PATTERN

OLYMPIC CHAMPION

Student's Name

"I press on toward the goal to win the prize for which God has called me."
Philippians 3:14

Group Leader's Name

Date

Grades 1 & 2

Miracles and Parables

Memory Verse: "I am the way, the truth, and the life: no man cometh unto the Father, but by Me."
John 14:6

IDEA Acting out some of the events in the life of Jesus can be a good learning experience for your students and make for enjoyable activities. You can use this get-together idea to help teach the boys and girls why Jesus came.

PUBLICITY

Fill in the details on the pattern to make invitations and enlarge to make a poster. To draw more attention to the poster, set it inside a basket placed on a table. Cut out a few fish shapes and place these around the basket.

DECORATIONS & PREPARATION

Use leftover teaching resources to cut out pictures of Jesus with people and hang these around the room. Decorate the serving table with various baskets; in the center place a good-sized picture of Jesus with children or of Jesus feeding the 5,000.

ACTIVITIES

Lead the Blind

What you'll need: Blindfolds and poster board or chalkboard

Group the students into pairs of two; blindfold one of the children in the each pair. The one who can still see will guide his partner across the room toward a helper who is playing the role of Jesus. When the pair reaches the helper, "Jesus" will remove the blindfold and the two students can turn around and run back to the starting line.

After all the children have participated in the role-playing game, read the story of blind Bartimaeus' encounter with Jesus told in Mark 10:46-52. Then have the boys and girls sing the following song to the tune of "Here We Go 'Round the Mulberry Bush." To make it easier for the chil-

dren, write out the words on a chalkboard or piece of poster board ahead of time.

> The blind man wanted to see again,
> To see again, to see again.
> The blind man wanted to see again,
> And so he called to Jesus.
>
> Jesus heard the blind man's cry,
> The blind man's cry, the blind man's cry.
> Jesus heard the blind man's cry,
> And helped him see again.

Find the Lost Lambs

What you'll need: Duplicated "Lost Lamb" puzzle and Jesus or lamb stickers

Ahead of time, duplicate a puzzle sheet for each child expected to come. At the meeting, read the parable of the lost sheep found in Matthew 18:12-14 before you hand out the puzzles. Emphasize with the boys and girls the idea that Jesus cares about every one of us. He doesn't want any of us to be lost.

Let the children work on the puzzles as long as necessary. Place a sticker on each child's paper as he finishes.

Goin' Fishin'

What you'll need: Table covered with blanket or tablecloth or a puppet stage, dowel rods, string, clothespins, plastic sandwich bags, and gel-type candy (Gummy Fish®, for example)

Make "fishing rods" for the children by tying one end of string to a dowel rod and the other end to a clothespin. The children will go "fishing" by throwing the line over the covered table or puppet stage, behind which a helper is waiting to "hook" the fish. When the clothespin comes over to the other side, the helper will attach a bag of candy and toss the "fish" back over.

When all the children have had the opportunity to go fishing, read to them the story of the miraculous catch of fish as told in Luke 5:1-11.

REFRESHMENTS

Following the previous activity, make a transition to refreshment time by relating the account of the feeding of the 5,000. Refer to John 6:1-13 for the story.

As your helpers serve fish sticks, warm rolls, and punch, talk with the children about how the little boy gave what he had, even though it wasn't very much, to help the Lord Jesus. He was willing to serve the Lord in whatever way he could. Ask, **What are some things we can do to show God that we are serving Him?**

DEVOTIONS

The actual devotional time will be brief, since much of the teaching has already taken place. Review the Bible lessons introduced in the other activities, then read John 21:25. Ask the children to name any other stories about Jesus that they know.

Say the memory verse together. Share with the students that the reason Jesus performed all the miracles and told all the parables He did was to show those around Him that He was really the Son of God. Jesus was sent to earth to save man from sin; He is the only one who could do the things He did. He is the only one who can show us the true way to God.

Close with prayer, praising Jesus for all the wonderful things He did while He was on earth and thanking Him for what He does for us today.

INVITATION

Little Lost Lambs

These little lambs need your help. They are lost in the bushes. Can you find them? Draw a circle around each lamb that you find. There are twenty lambs.

Dilly-Dally Double Day

Memory Verse: "A friend loves at all times." Proverbs 17:17 (NIV)

IDEA As "two heads are better than one," this plan goes all out for a terrific time for twosomes. The children will enjoy cooperating with each other in the various games. They will also learn to appreciate the value of friendship, especially with their best friend, Jesus.

PUBLICITY

Duplicate the invitation pattern after you have filled in the details. Make an enlarged copy for the poster, perhaps creating two posters to tack up side by side.

When making announcements in class, you might try repeating the words you say!

DECORATIONS & PREPARATION

Gather used magazines and leftover teaching resources to find pictures of people doing things together, preferably in pairs. Cut out these pictures and duplicate; hang them as mobiles from the ceiling or display together on the walls.

Try to set up two of everything on the serving table.

For prizes use two-for-one coupons for area restaurants and stores.

ACTIVITIES

Choosing Pairs
What you'll need: Large container

As the children arrive, have each guest take off one shoe and place it in a large box or other container. If you have an uneven number, make sure to throw in the shoe of a helper at the beginning of the drawing.

When all have arrived, gather around the box while two helpers take turns drawing out shoes. The owners of the two shoes drawn will be a pair for the duration of the party. Continue drawing out shoes, making pairs, until each guest is paired up.

Couple Contests
What you'll need: Handkerchiefs, bandannas, or strips of fabric from an old sheet

Three-legged Race
Have the children stand in pairs side by side and tie their inside legs together. At the signal, all couples will race a predetermined distance and return to the starting point.

Blind Buddy Race
Keep the pairs tied together as in the previous race and blindfold one member of the pair. You may want to complicate the race by having a curved course or placing soft obstacles in the way. Have three or four couples at a time compete.

Couple Obstacle Course
Set up an obstacle course and let the pairs run it tied loosely together either at the arms or legs.

Spider Run
Tie the pair's inside arms and legs together and have them drop to "all sixes," then race.

Pinkie Pennies
What you'll need: Pennies

Partners should stand facing each other and place a penny between their little fingers on each hand. They will try to walk together sideways to the finish line.

It's a Toss-Up
What you'll need: Supplies will vary

A variety of contests can be held with the pairs tossing things back and forth. Begin with the students standing just a few feet apart, then have them take one step backward after each successful toss. The winning couple is the last one to remain after all others have dropped their object, or the couple farthest apart after a time limit of a few minutes.

A few ideas would include water balloons, eggs, pennies, paper airplanes, wadded paper, potatoes, frisbees, marshmallows, bean bags, and tennis balls.

Creative Couples

What you'll need: Slips of paper, a container, blindfold, sheets of paper, and pencils

Write down a few suggestions of things for the children to draw, such as a house, car, dog, cat, telephone, etc. and put these slips into a container. Blindfold one member of each pair and give him a sheet of paper, pencil, and something solid to write on. The other partner will take a slip out of the container and, without telling his partner the name of what he is drawing, give instructions on how to draw a picture of the object. After all contestants have had a turn, vote on the picture that looks most like the object named.

REFRESHMENTS

Have a food fest with goodies that come in double packages, peanuts in their shells, and/or double-decker sandwiches. Provide "two-ty fruity punch" to drink.

DEVOTIONS

Read Ecclesiastes 4:9-10 and talk about how people cooperating together can get more accomplished than just one; use examples familiar to the children, such as washing dishes.

Invite the children to say aloud the names of their friends — they may include schoolmates as well as church pals. Ask them to share what they like about their friendships. Discuss with the students that friends not only help us, but they also talk and listen, share, and play with us.

Say, **Jesus wants to be our Friend, too. He cares about us like no one else can. He will always be there to talk and listen, because He loves us.**

Repeat the memory verse with the students, then sing "What A Friend We Have In Jesus." Close with prayer.

INVITATION

Red, White, and Blue Fair

Memory Verse: "If the Son therefore shall make you free, ye shall be free indeed." John 8:36

IDEA In early America the fair provided a chance for playing games, eating food, and displaying handiwork. Plan a modern-day fair to help celebrate the country's special day. Your students will find out what freedom means to a Christian.

PUBLICITY

Begin publicizing the fair at least one month before it is scheduled in order to give the children ample time to prepare their products to exhibit.

Write in the details on the pattern and duplicate to make invitations. Make up a list of the exhibit categories (see Preparation) and duplicate to go along with the invitation.

Enlarge the pattern or use a large sheet of white poster board to make a poster. Color in the title appropriately. Include any details the parents will want to know, such as what to bring for the picnic (see Refreshments) or whether to bring lounge chairs. Also include the list of exhibit categories.

DECORATIONS & PREPARATION

This is definitely an outdoor event, so plan to hold it at a park, playground, picnic area, or your church grounds and parking lot. Elaborate decorations are not necessary, but you need to plan areas for the display booths. If the church grounds are used you could set up the exhibits indoors.

Game tables and other folding tables would be ideal, or mark areas with red, white, and blue crepe paper streamers and set the items on blankets on the ground. Have a sign prepared for each category planned.

Choose as many of the categories listed below as you feel will interest your students. Add others that they request. The suggested categories would include: handcrafts or needlecrafts, art, baking, gardening, and collections (stuffed animals, stick-ers, stamps, baseball cards, etc.). Each student may enter as many exhibits, and as many entries in each category, as he desires.

Use red, white, and blue suckers, gumballs, and other candy as prizes in the games.

If it is feasible, a fitting climax for this event would be to attend a fireworks display in your community.

ACTIVITIES

Fair Exhibits

What you'll need: Duplicated entry cards, pencils, duplicated "ribbons," and other materials (see Preparation)

Ahead of time, duplicate the award ribbons; make the first place blue, second place red, third place yellow, and honorable mention white. Duplicate the pattern for the entry cards and pass these out to the children as they arrive with their items. The filled out card should be placed underneath the item when it is exhibited so it will not show during the judging.

Choose a helper and a parent as judges of each exhibit. Parents should not judge categories their children have entered. After the judging is completed, attach the appropriate ribbons to the entries and display the name cards of all the exhibitors. (Honorable mention should be used for all entries other than the first, second, and third place winners.)

Red, White, and Blue Race

What you'll need: Red, white, and blue rags, rope, and cardboard tubes

Tie a long rope between two trees or have two helpers hold it about three feet from the ground. Tie red, white, and blue rags or scraps of fabric loosely to the rope—one set of rags for each team of three participants.

Stand the teams about twenty-five feet from the rope and give each team a cardboard tube such as what is used for paper towels or wrapping paper. At the "go" signal, the first person on each team should run toward the rope holding the tube. He will untie a red streamer from the rope and tie it back on his cardboard tube. He will then run back to his team and hand the tube to the second player, who runs to the rope, unties a white rag and ties it onto the tube. The third player will do the same with the blue rag.

As soon as all three colors are on the team's cardboard tube, the members must sit down behind the starting line. The first team to do so wins.

Three-Legged Race
What you'll need: Handkerchiefs

Divide the group into pairs. Have each couple stand side by side and help them tie their inside legs together with one handkerchief at the ankles and another just below the knees. At the starting signal the three-legged couples must run a given distance, turn around and run back again.

Sack Relay
What you'll need: Burlap sacks

Divide the group into as many equal teams as you have sacks. At the starting signal the first participant should step inside the sack and hop to the finish line. He should then climb out of the sack and run with it back to the next player on his team, who repeats the action. The relay continues until all the members of one team have hopped and returned.

Flag Tag
What you'll need: Red, white, and blue rags

Use the rags or pieces of fabric from the Red, White, and Blue Race *or* tear an old sheet into pieces about eight inches long and two inches wide. With marking pens, color one-third of the pieces blue and one-third red, leaving one-third white.

Divide the group into three equal teams—the reds, the whites, and the blues. Give each team its color of rags. Each player tucks one rag into the back of his belt, waistband or back pocket with most of the rag dangling accessibly down his leg.

Give the players about ten seconds to scatter about the playing area. At the command "go," each player should try to grab someone else's "flag" (of

INVITATION

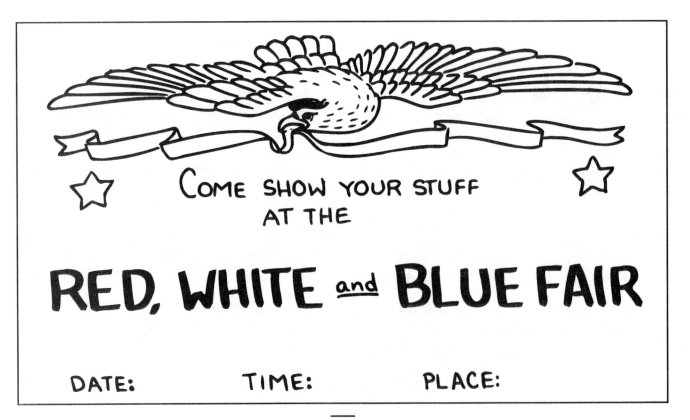

COME SHOW YOUR STUFF
AT THE

RED, WHITE and BLUE FAIR

DATE: TIME: PLACE:

a different color), yet keep his own flag. A player may watch from the sidelines after he loses his flag. When all the flags of two teams have been taken, the teams may reassemble and count their flags. The team having the most flags in its possession is the winner.

REFRESHMENTS

If you are at a park or some other location where you can barbecue, cook up some good old fashioned hamburgers and hot dogs. The families can bring various salads, chips, and relish trays. Provide canned soft drinks or red fruit punch. Save the dessert for the next activity.

Watermelon Eating Contest

Cut semi-circle slices of watermelon for each participant. Let each contestant set his piece of melon on the table and stand or sit behind it with hands behind his back. At the "go" signal the participants may begin eating. The first one to eat to the rind is the winner and is rewarded with another piece of watermelon!

Cut up the rest of the melon for everyone to share.

DEVOTIONS

You might want to take the opportunity to teach the children a number of patriotic songs. The boys and girls will enjoy having their parents sing with them. Some suggestions would include "Yankee Doodle," "America the Beautiful," and perhaps even the "Star-Spangled Banner."

After the sing-along time, talk with the students about the meaning of freedom. Ask, **What does it mean if something is free?** (We do not have to pay for it, all we have to do is take it.)

Tell your listeners that the Bible also talks about freedom. Explain that when we disobey God, that is called sin. The punishment for sin is death, but God sent His Son, Jesus, to die for us instead. Read Romans 6:23. Say, **A gift is free, isn't it? To accept God's free gift, all we have to do is ask Him to forgive us of our sins. I John 1:9 says that if we ask God to cleanse us and forgive us, He will. That is how we can be free.**

Say the memory verse with the children, then invite them to pray. Watch for possible signs that they are ready to take the step of accepting Jesus as Savior and be prepared to follow through.

PATTERN FOR DUPLICATION

45

Pick Up Project

Memory Verse: "Thus saith the Lord, The heaven is my throne, and the earth is my footstool." Isaiah 66:1

IDEA

Getting your group together bright and early some morning to help clean up the environment will be an innovative activity. While the children are taking part in the project, they will learn the importance of keeping God's world beautiful for everyone.

PUBLICITY

Use a toy pick-up truck or dump truck as an advertising piece. Make a sign for the back of the truck (a "sign post" stuck in a lump of play dough) by duplicating the pattern provided and including the date, time, and place to meet. Fill the truck with scraps of paper, sticks, wrappers, etc. Set the truck on a table several weeks ahead of the project date.

DECORATIONS & PREPARATION

The main activities for this get-together will be cleaning up and collecting, so decorations are not necessary.

For preparation, find out how your group could participate in some recycling projects in the community.

Choose a project or two that you could handle, then make the necessary arrangements:

• Cleaning up a park—Find a spot that needs attention or plan to go to several locations. Make the necessary contacts with authorities.

• Collection projects—These can be tackled in several ways. One is to announce to your congregation that your class will be collecting newspapers, plastic, and aluminum cans, etc., and ask for the addresses of homes where members would like to participate in your project.

Another is to choose several neighborhoods to cover and distribute fliers listing what and when you will be collecting. You can either have community residents bring their recyclable items to you or drive through the neighborhoods on a specified day and pick up the materials. You would then need to round up several pick-up trucks or station wagons and drivers to take the children to the homes.

Once you have gathered the materials, you will need a location to deliver them for recycling. Many agencies will pay your group for the recyclable items, so this aspect of the project could be a fund raiser as well.

ACTIVITIES

Begin the get-together with breakfast (see Refreshments). When ready, assign the children to teams with adult leaders/drivers, then give instructions for the morning's activities depending on what projects you have chosen. Set time limits, assign locations, and tell everyone what procedures are to be followed.

As you transport the group to the park area or to the neighborhoods, keep in mind that having children sit in the back of a truck is not safe and is illegal in many states.

Park Pick-Up
What you'll need: Plastic trash bags, plastic gloves, and paper grocery sacks

Give each team a couple of plastic trash bags with twist ties for the waste and one paper sack to keep aluminum cans; provide plastic gloves for the children to wear. Send the groups off to systematically cover the grounds. If you wish, make a game of it by challenging the children to see who can collect the most (no leaves or rocks allowed!).

Caution: stick to areas where there are no traffic hazards. Picking up debris along a roadside or highway is dangerous.

Recyclables Collection

What you'll need: Paper grocery sacks

Much of the work for this activity will have already taken place with the planning, preparation, and publicity. Keep a supply of paper sacks on hand in case you need to bag some items. If you'll be at a drop-off site, you might want to have helpers play games with the children during the "lull" times. If you receive payment for bringing in the recyclable items, be sure to tell the children how much money they raised.

REFRESHMENTS

On the day you choose to have this activity, make your first stop at a park or picnic area and serve a "tailgate" breakfast from the trucks and station wagons. If there are cooking facilities, try making egg sandwiches—scrambled eggs on English muffins with a slice of melted cheese. Serve with fruit slices and milk. If no cooking facilities are available, serve doughnuts and milk or juice.

DEVOTIONS

When your tasks are done (allowing perhaps the entire morning) and your "collections" are properly taken care of, gather the children together for a time of sharing.

Talk with the boys and girls about the wonder of creation. Encourage them to use their senses to experience its beauty—by running their toes in the grass, smelling a bed of flowers, listening to the song of a blue jay, and so on.

Say, **God created the world as a beautiful place for us to live. We need to take care of the earth so that others can enjoy it, too. That's why we did the project today.**

Read Psalm 24:1-2 and then lead the children in singing "This is My Father's World." Repeat the memory verse and close with a prayer and praise circle, thanking God for the opportunity to help take care of His beautiful world.

INVITATION

KEEP AMERICA BEAUTIFUL!

Student's Name

was a key member of the Pick Up Project.

Group Leader's Name

Date

Treasure Hunt

Memory Verse: "Lay up for yourselves treasures in heaven, where neither moth nor rust doth corrupt." Matthew 6:20

IDEA
The excitement of a treasure hunt coupled with fun games and refreshments offers a get-together few primaries could resist! In addition to the fun, the children will discover what it means to give God our best.

PUBLICITY
Fill in the details on the pattern provided. Duplicate to make invitations and enlarge to make a poster. For a dramatic effect, glue on some circles of gold and/or silver wrapping paper.

DECORATIONS & PREPARATION
As this will be an outdoor event you will not need special decorations, but a bit more preparation is in order. Your first task will be to make a "treasure chest" filled with wrapped goodies for your students to hunt for and share.

The treasure chest can be a shoe box, a fishing tackle box, or a metal cash box decorated to look like a treasure chest. It could be covered with foil or shiny adhesive-backed plastic. Strapping or chest hinges could be simulated by using black electrical tape.

Collect or buy an assortment of inexpensive costume jewelry. Glue it to the top of the box so that it looks like a real treasure chest.

The wrapped items in the buried chest can be pieces of bubble gum or penny candy, marbles, balloons, candy bars, or numerous other things you can find in a novelty store.

ACTIVITIES
Treasure Hunt
What you'll need: Treasure chest (see Preparation) and clues

Decide how many teams you will have and make a treasure map for each team. Use different colored paper on which to write the clues for each team. Make the directions simple, such as "Go to the tree next to the trash can and look closely at the branches." Each clue should lead the children to another clue until the last one leads them to the actual treasure chest.

Clues may be hidden in a variety of places—pinned to a branch of a low-hanging tree, fastened to the underside of a bush, hidden in the end of a hollow log, stuffed inside a paper bag, etc. Be sure that clues are not placed in dangerous locations.

At "Treasure Hunt" time, take the children to the area where the treasure is "hidden" and give each team its first clue. Whichever team finds the treasure first may open the box and dig in to the goodies, then share with the rest of the children.

Backward Walk
What you'll need: Room to play

Mark off an unobstructed course, about twenty-five feet long, for the teams and line them up. Walking backwards, the children will race against each other from the *end* of the course to the *beginning.* The hitch is that if anyone turns around to see how he is coming within the course, he must start over. Teammates should make no sounds, but may indicate with their hands if a walker is getting too far off course to arrive at the beginning line.

As soon as the first member of the team has arrived at the beginning, the second member in line may begin the walk. The first team finished wins.

Pieces of Eight Hunt

What you'll need: Pennies, foil gift wrap, and chocolate foil-wrapped coins (optional)

Ahead of time, individually wrap eight pennies for each team in foil gift wrapping paper—red, gold, green, silver, etc. Hide the pennies around the ground, being sure they can be found without having to dig.

At the signal all teams may begin hunting for their pieces of eight. Remind them to collect only their own color coins. The first team to find them all may be awarded chocolate foil-wrapped coins to hand out to each other and then to the other guests.

REFRESHMENTS

Serve cupcakes with hidden treasures in them, such as a cream filling, along with punch.

DEVOTIONS

(Relate the following to the children):

After the discovery of America, great sailing ships made the journey from Spain to the New World carrying back loads of gold and silver. Many of the great ships were sunk in storms at sea and in battles with the gunboats of other nations. People still search for the treasures, hoping to become fabulously rich through a lucky find.

King David of Israel gathered one of the greatest treasures ever collected in one place. He wanted to build a great temple for the Lord, but God told David his son, Solomon, should build it instead. For many years, then, David worked on collecting all the materials for his son to do the actual building. I Chronicles 22:14 tells us how much gold and silver David gathered to use in the building of the temple. *(Read the verse.)* **That works out to about 3,750 tons of gold and 37, 500 tons of silver!**

Why did David gather so many materials for the temple? Because he wanted the house of God to have the very best. God deserves our best today, too. What are some ways that we can show God we are giving Him our best? *(Doing schoolwork, giving an offering, helping a friend, etc.)*

It doesn't matter how big our allowance is, or how many softball trophies or good citizen certificates we have. We might "treasure" these kinds of things for a while, but they will not last. What we do for God will last. God is pleased when we give Him our best, and He will reward us in heaven.

(Close the devotional time by saying the memory verse with the children and then praying that they would give their best to God.)

INVITATION

Grades 3 & 4

Dipsy Doodle Day

Memory Verse: "Always be prepared to give an answer to everyone who asks you to give the reason for the hope that you have." I Peter 3:15 (NIV)

IDEA
This activity involves the unlikely pair of fun with water and fun with drawing. Just as your students will be inquisitive about the title, they will learn that their friends are curious about what being a Christian means.

PUBLICITY

Write in the date, time, and place on the invitation pattern. Enlarge the invitation to make a poster. Decorate with a few star stickers and tape on several pencils and a small ladle.

DECORATIONS & PREPARATION

Make stars to hang from the ceiling and use your imagination to draw doodle pictures with stick figures to hang on the walls.

Award decorative pencils, souvenir spoons, and/or sheets of star stickers as prizes.

ACTIVITIES

Big Dipper
What you'll need: Two buckets, measuring cup, pitcher, chair or step stool, water, and score sheet

To play this outdoor game, place a bucket on the ground with an empty measuring cup in the center of the bucket. Next to the bucket place a sturdy chair. Fill a second bucket with water for the "reservoir."

Each contestant will stand on the chair, and, holding a pitcher of water at eye level, see how much water he can manage to pour into the cup in 30 seconds. Keep a tally of how much each student gets and award prizes to the top three.

Doodle Charades
What you'll need: Several dozen sheets of paper, pencils, and something to write on

Divide the group evenly into small groups of three or four. Give each group a dozen sheets of paper, pencils, and something to write on.

Each group is to choose a representative who will go to the other end of the room or a different room if possible. When all the representatives are there, tell them the name of a song or book you are sure anyone in the group would recognize. Each representative will then go back to his group and try to draw out the song or book on the paper. He may not use words or symbols, and he may speak only when the group guesses the title correctly. The first group to guess the title receives five points.

Send a different person from each group each time. The first group to reach twenty-five points wins.

Keep Dipping!
What you'll need: Paper cups, one quart of water, and one empty quart container

Divide into two or more teams, and give each team member a paper cup. Place a full quart carton of water on the floor at the beginning of the line and an empty quart container at the end.

At a given signal, the first team member will fill his paper cup with water from the carton, then pour the water from his cup into the cup of the next person in line. Repeat the procedure all the way down the line to the last contestant, who will pour the contents of his cup into the empty container. He then calls out, "Keep dipping!" and the first person in line fills his cup and the relay starts again. Continue until one team has emptied the carton and the last drop has gone into the container.

The winning team won't necessarily be the first team finished, but the one which ends up with the most water in the container.

Dipper Doodle Relay

What you'll need: Two large sheets of plain paper, masking tape, and markers

Tape the two sheets of paper at the children's shoulder level several feet apart on a wall. Keep the same teams as the last game. Line both teams up five feet from the wall and provide markers.

Each team tries to draw the best "doodle picture" (the picture can be anything). Each member of the team can only draw one line on the picture and then must run back to his team and hand the marking pen to the next person in line. The teams may confer for a minute before starting. Determine the winning picture on the basis of speed and quality.

REFRESHMENTS

Provide a variety of chips and several different dips. If desired, you could also make finger sandwiches. Serve punch from a large bowl and use a big dipper!

DEVOTIONS

(Gather the children into a quiet circle and discuss the following):

When you came to the party, most of you had no idea what a "Dipsy Doodle" day was. Maybe you still don't! But after all the dipping and doodling, it probably makes some sense to you by now.

Perhaps to some of your friends at school the word "Christian" means about as much to them as "dipsy doodle" did to you. They really don't know what a Christian is. If we were to ask them to define a Christian, we might get a lot of different answers.

When you go to school, you will probably tell your friends about the "Dipsy Doodle" day and the fun we had—and you will more than likely have to explain what it was all about. Do you think you could also tell those same friends what it means to ask Jesus into their hearts? The Bible says we should always be ready to share with others about the love of God, to tell them that He loves us so much that He sent His Son to take our punishment for our wrongdoing (I Peter 3:15). God's Word also says, though, that if we are ashamed of the Lord, He will be ashamed of us (Luke 9:26).

How can you help others ask Jesus into their lives?

Let's say the memory verse together and then pray that God would give us the courage to share His Good News with our friends.

INVITATION

Silly Sticks and Stuff

Memory Verse: "The Lord will fulfill His purpose for me; Your love, O Lord, endures forever." Psalm 138:8 (NIV)

IDEA

Take a trip to the mountains or woods (or at least a nearby park) so you can find enough "resources" for this interesting activity. In addition to playing some out-of-the-ordinary games, the children will see how God can use us in not-so-ordinary ways.

PUBLICITY

Write in the date, time, and place on the invitation pattern and duplicate. If you hand deliver the invitations, tape on a toothpick for effect.

For a "poster," partially fill a bucket with mud and cover the top with clear plastic wrap. Poke a large stick through the plastic and attach a sign to it with the following words: DON'T BE A STICK-IN-THE-MUD. Include an invitation underneath.

DECORATIONS & PREPARATION

Make arrangements for transportation. Make sure you have all the necessary equipment with you. For Refreshments you will need a place where you can build a fire or barbecue.

ACTIVITIES

Mini-Stick Relay
What you'll need: Two dozen toothpicks and two matchboxes or envelopes

Divide the group into relay teams and give each team a dozen toothpicks in a matchbox or envelope. Set up a goal line about twenty-five feet away.

The first person on each team must run to the appointed place, dump out the toothpicks, and return to his team. He will hand the empty box or envelope to the next person, who will run up to retrieve the toothpicks, replacing them in the container.

The last person in line must count the toothpicks to be sure there are still twelve. If some are missing, the player must go to the area where they were dumped and try to find the lost ones. The first team to present its box of twelve toothpicks is the winner. Give peppermint sticks for prizes.

Broomstick Jump
What you'll need: A broomstick

Have two helpers hold a broomstick about a foot off the ground. The children will take turns jumping over the stick. The holders may gradually raise the stick between jumpers, eliminating players who cannot jump over the stick at the new height, until only the best stick jumper is left. Give him the "Great Jumping Bean Award"—a "medal" with a real Mexican jumping bean or another bean of some sort glued on it.

Next, the children will take turns going under the stick, bending backwards. The holders will keep lowering the stick, thus eliminating those who cannot get under it, until one player is left. Give him the "Great Pretzel Award" to hang around his neck in the form of a pretzel tied on a ribbon.

Stick Ball
What you'll need: Two broomsticks and two balls

Divide the group into two teams. Place half of each team on either side of two lines about 30 feet apart. Give the first person on each team a broomstick and a basketball or volleyball. At the go signal the line leader will run toward the other half of his team, hitting the ball in front of him with the stick. When he reaches the line, he will give the stick to that line leader, who will then hit the ball back to the starting line.

Continue the game until one team has run all of its members twice with the ball, thus putting them back into their original positions. Award the team with pretzel sticks.

REFRESHMENTS

The refreshments will be fruit punch and anything that can be cooked over a fire. The old standbys, of course, are hot dogs and marshmallows.

Unless the children can sit around the fire, be sure to estinguish it before you begin the devotional.

DEVOTIONS

As the children settle down for devotions, display a few sticks of various sizes and shapes. Ask the boys and girls to use their imaginations to think of how the sticks could be used. They might come up with some interesting things!

To focus on the scriptural lesson, talk to the students about a very special stick from the Bible. This was the rod, or staff, of Moses.

Say, **The rod of Moses was just like any other in that day, except for one thing: The Lord God used it to show His mighty power. When Moses listened to the Lord, miraculous things happened.**

Turn to several passages that relate some of these events: In the calling of Moses, his rod turns into a snake and then back again (Exodus 4:1-5). The plague of blood comes upon Egypt when Moses strikes the Nile River with his rod (Exodus 7:19-24). As Pharaoh and his army are fast approaching, Moses stretches his rod over the Red Sea and the Israelites cross over on dry ground (Exodus 14:21-27). When Moses strikes a rock, water comes gushing out for the thirsty people (Exodus 17:3-7).

Ask the children, **Was there anything special about the rod itself?** (No, the power came from God.) **Why do you think God used the stick in so many ways?** (To honor Himself and to show His power.)

Emphasize to the boys and girls that no matter who we are, God can do great things with us. By choosing to follow the Lord, we can encourage a friend, help a teacher, or do any number of special things for God. He has a purpose in mind for us. The important thing is to ask Him to live in us and do what He thinks is best.

Say the memory verse with the guests, then offer a closing prayer asking God to guide the children as they find out His purpose for them.

INVITATION

Out-Of-Sight Overnighter

Memory Verse: " All Thy works shall praise Thee, O Lord; and Thy saints shall bless Thee... and talk of Thy power." Psalm 145:10-11

IDEA Take your students camping! Getting away for a while to feel the fresh air and play in the "great outdoors" will remind the boys and girls to praise God for His tremendous creation.

PUBLICITY

Fill in the details on the pattern and duplicate to make invitations. It might be a good idea to also distribute a flier giving the details as to where to meet, what kind of clothing to have along, what other equipment is needed, when you will get back, etc. Send the Pre-Registration and Medical Release Form along with the invitation (see Preparation).

Make a large poster to publicize the outing as well. Include all the information listed above.

DECORATIONS & PREPARATION

Set aside a Friday night and Saturday for the event. Allow at least a month for planning, making advance arrangements, and gathering equipment.

Site—Select a campsite at least an hour away from the church so the group can really feel like it is "getting away from it all." Look for a site with outdoor cooking and sanitary facilities. Be sure to make reservations.

Equipment—Depending on the campsite, you will need some sizeable cabin tents, portable stoves, lanterns and fuel, ice chests, a first aid kit, and firewood. Be sure you know all the fire regulations and have arranged for a permit, if needed. You will also need some game equipment such as softballs, bats, a kickball, Frisbees®, etc., and several table games.

Each person should bring his own sleeping bag or blankets and pillow in addition to a change of clothes, toiletries, jacket, flashlight, and Bible.

Registration and Cost—Duplicate the Pre-Registration and Medical Release Form for your students to turn in at least two weeks in advance. Be as firm as possible in getting commitments by the deadline but be prepared for last-minute additions.

Determine the cost based upon expenses for the campsite and food; try to keep it as low as possible. Perhaps your church has a fund available to help offset the cost. The children should turn in their money with the registration form.

Additional Helpers—Enlist adequate adult helpers for transportation, food preparation, and general supervision. Help is especially important for this kind of loosely-structured, overnight activity.

ACTIVITIES

Friday Evening

Leave early enough so you can set up camp while it is still light. Assign one or two adult helpers per tent and help everyone unload their gear. When all are settled, have dinner (see Refreshments). Let the children help in preparation and clean-up.

Spend some time playing games after the meal. If it is already dark, a game of flashlight tag might be fun. Be sure to confine the children to a specific area when playing any nighttime game. A helper should build a campfire at this time.

As the children assemble around the campfire, start singing some of their favorite camp songs, leading them gradually into quiet choruses. After spending time in God's Word (see Devotions), the children may enjoy a snack time (see Refreshments).

If the restroom facilities are some distance away, have helpers accompany the children for one last trek before turning in. Let the children sleep until they wake up on their own the next morning.

Saturday Morning

After the group has eaten and cleaned up (see Refreshments), have a praise time (see Devotions).

Next, go on a hike, perhaps to collect leaves or rocks. Plan your hike ahead of time, if possible, so you will have a destination in mind and will know how much time to allow.

After returning to the campsite, play some group games and run a few simple races and relays before going on a Comparison Scavenger Hunt. Divide the group into teams of two or three, with an adult helper. Depending on the size of your play area, allow about ten minutes for the groups to gather the following items:
1. The biggest piece of wood they can find
2. The heaviest rock
3. The biggest leaf
4. The brightest flower
5. The straightest branch
6. The smelliest sock
7. The longest blade of grass
8. The cleanest comb

Blow a whistle to signify the start and stop times. Have a representative from each group bring the items up for comparison as they are called.

Saturday Afternoon

Direct the boys and girls to wash up for lunch (see Refreshments). After eating and cleaning up, the afternoon's activities will vary according to the facilities that are available. You might want to play softball or kickball, go swimming, ride horses, etc. Or play some individual or small team sports such as badminton, croquet, archery, and so on.

The helpers should enter into the sports and play activities so the children will be well-supervised. Allow about two hours for this period of recreation.

By mid-afternoon the group should be ready to return home. When all the gear has been loaded up, clean up the grounds (a good incentive is to ask that everything be left *better* than when you arrived). Gather everyone together for a closing prayer, then head for home. Make sure all the equipment gets back to the right owners.

REFRESHMENTS

You will need to prepare for three full meals–Friday dinner, Saturday breakfast, and Saturday

INVITATION

YOU ARE INVITED TO AN

Out-of-Sight Overnighter!

DATES:

PLACE:

COST:

lunch–and a snack for the campfire on Friday night. **Here are some suggested menus:**

Friday Dinner
Beef and macaroni, celery and carrot sticks, cupcakes or fruit, milk

Friday Night Snack
Chips and dip, roasted marshmallows

Saturday Breakfast
Cold cereal, fresh fruit, cocoa or milk

Saturday Lunch
Hot dogs, pork and beans, potato chips, fruit punch, cookies

Make a list of everything necessary for each meal as well as items required for preparation and serving. Remember essentials such as skillets, a can opener, matches, and coffee for the adults!

DEVOTIONS

The devotions for the weekend will focus on praising God for His gift of creation.

Friday—Ask the children to focus on their surroundings. If you are away from the city, you will probably be able to see a great number of stars and perhaps even the Milky Way.

Read Psalm 19:1-6 and ask, **When the Bible says "the heavens declare the glory of God," what does that mean to you?** (Wait for their responses.) **All throughout Scripture, we can see that nature points to its Creator. Only God could make so many stars. He's the only One who could set the sun and moon in the sky, or create trees in a forest, or make the water in a stream flow. And because of that, God deserves our praise.**

Lead the children in singing "How Great Thou Art." Say the memory verse together and then pray.

Saturday—Begin the devotional time by having the boys and girls take turns reading Psalm 148. Ask, **What does it mean to praise the Lord?** (Wait for their responses.) **Praise is a part of worshipping God. We praise Him because He is so magnificent. Just look around you at the Lord's wonderful creation. He made all this for us.**

Read verse 12 again and note that children are to praise the Lord. Give the boys and girls opportunity to say what they would like to praise Him for.

Sing a praise song before repeating the memory verse. End the devotional time with prayer.

Out-Of-Sight Overnighter
Pre-Registration and Medical Release Form

Student's Name _____

Address _____

_____

Phone (   ) _____ Birthdate _____

Parent's Name & Phone _____

Someone to notify in an emergency other than the parent:

_____ Phone (   ) _____

I hereby give permission to the adult supervisors of _____

to seek medical help as necessary on the following dates _____

Insurance Co. _____ Policy # _____

Parent signature _____

I WAS SEEN

at the

OUT-OF-SIGHT OVERNIGHTER

"All Thy works shall praise Thee, O Lord."
Psalm 145:10

Student's Name

Date

Group Leader's Name

Freedom Celebration

Memory Verse: "By this shall all men know that ye are My disciples, if ye have love one to another." John 13:35

IDEA

As you celebrate the Fourth of July with your students, focus on one of its main ideas—freedom. You will be able to draw a parallel with the symbols of Christianity.

PUBLICITY

Fill in the information on the invitation pattern and duplicate.

To make a poster, cut a large shield from poster board. Across the top glue a strip of blue construction paper and scatter gummed stars on it. Below the star field, vertically glue strips of red construction paper to make a red and white striped design. Across these stripes print the details in large letters.

DECORATIONS & PREPARATION

Decorate with the traditional red, white, and blue. Use crepe paper, balloons, and anything else patriotic. Cut stars out of poster board and wrap with aluminum foil to hang from the ceiling or from trees.

For devotions, locate a picture of a dove with an olive branch. Draw the symbol of the fish (two half circles intersecting) and a cross.

ACTIVITIES

Uncle Sam's Socks

What you'll need: Red, white, and blue pairs of men's socks and three chairs

Give each team a pair of men's socks in the team color. Place a low chair twenty feet in front of the team. The first player will take the socks to the chair, put them on, run back to the team, take the socks off, and hand them to the next player. The first team to finish wins.

Statue of Liberty Tag

What you'll need: Room to play

Choose someone to be "It." Children will be safe and may not be tagged when they assume the pose of the Statue of Liberty—the right arm held high and the left arm holding an imaginary book. If the players fail to get the pose correct or "It" sneaks up on them, they can be tagged. Let several have a turn to be "It."

Potluck

What you'll need: Circle of chairs

For this game the starting player will begin by saying the name of a state and then a food that begins with the same letter, such as Florida French Fry. The person next to him will say another state and food, perhaps California Cantaloupe. No one may repeat a state or food that has already been named.

Stripe Stripping

What you'll need: Crepe paper and blunt scissors for each team

Every other person on each team will need a strip of crepe paper in his team's color. The strips should be about two inches wide and three feet long. The first two players on each team will work together to cut their paper lengthwise; one person will hold the strip while the other cuts it. Then they will pass the scissors to the next two, who will cut theirs, and so on.

The first team finished wins. Use strips as decorations.

Star-Rippers

What you'll need: Construction paper

Give each guest a sheet of construction paper. Award a prize to the boy and girl who *tear* the best-shaped star. Papers may be folded to help make lines straighter, but no pencil outlines are allowed!

REFRESHMENTS

Serve "red, white, and blueberry sundaes"—scoops of vanilla and strawberry ice cream with fresh blueberries or blueberry jam. Top with whipped cream and a cherry.

DEVOTIONS

Talk with the children about the various symbols of freedom in the United States. Say, **We have played some games with stars and stripes today. When we see stars and stripes, we think of our country. Can you think of other things that represent our nation?** (The bald eagle, Uncle Sam, the Liberty Bell, the Statue of Liberty, etc.) Tell the children, **The world can look at these expressions of the United States.**

Explain to the boys and girls that Christianity has symbols too. Can they tell what some of them are? Say, **When we see a picture of a dove with an olive branch in its mouth, it stands for peace. In John 14:27, Jesus says that He gives us a peace that the world cannot give.**

Another symbol is the design of a fish. Explain that the Christians of the early church used the fish as sort of a secret code to protect themselves from people who wanted to hurt them. Say, **When someone drew one-half of a fish with a stick on the ground, he would know the other person was a Christian if that man drew the second half of the fish. In calling some of His disciples, who were fishermen, Jesus said He would make them "fishers of men."** We still use the fish symbol today to show that we are witnesses of the love of Christ.

Tell the boys and girls that a third symbol is a very important one—the symbol of the cross. Made out of trees, the cross was used by the Romans as a way to kill criminals. Tell the children, **Jesus was killed as if He was a common thief, but He broke the power of death. Both His cross and His grave are empty because Jesus came back to life! He is alive now, and His Spirit lives in our hearts when we invite Him in.**

An often unspoken symbol of our Christian walk is the love we express to others. Jesus said, "By this shall all men know that ye are My disciples, if ye have love one to another" (John 13:35). Say this verse with the boys and girls, then pray with them that we would readily show our faith to others.

INVITATION

Summer Safari

Memory Verse: *"God shall supply all your need according to His riches in glory by Christ Jesus."*
Philippians 4:19

IDEA
A "jungle adventure" is sure to snap your students out of the summer doldrums. By the safari's end the guests will see how much God cares for His creation.

PUBLICITY
Duplicate the invitation pattern after you have filled in the details. To brighten up the invitations, color the grass. For a poster, enlarge the pattern and add pictures of wild animals cut from old magazines.

DECORATIONS & PREPARATION
Use lots of green crepe paper to create a jungle atmosphere. Hang two-foot long strips from the ceiling. Make a tree by setting a broom upside down in a coffee can filled with sand; bunch up green crepe paper around the broom end. Have a few stuffed animals, preferably "jungle-types," in prominent places around the room.

ACTIVITIES

Jumbled Jungle
What you'll need: Duplicated animal shapes, scissors, envelopes, and tape

Ahead of time duplicate the wild animal patterns so you have several copies of each. Cut the patterns in two pieces, jigsaw puzzle fashion.

Hand out the animal puzzles in envelopes along with pieces of tape. Allow two or three minutes for the guests to match up their puzzles. When you give the signal that time is up, those who have not found the rest of their animals must match up with the person nearest them. You may end up with an "ele-potamus!"

Little Game Hunt
What you'll need: Empty jars and an ice pick or other tool to punch holes with

For this activity the children will turn into "hunters," searching for wildlife such as ants, beetles, grasshoppers, and other harmless insects.

For those who do not care to "hunt," ask for a group of volunteers to make the "cages." Provide a few jars with lids which you have punched holes in ahead of time. The children may search for grass and twigs to put in the jars.

The other guests may seek out and capture the "wild game." Allow ten minutes or so for both groups to complete their tasks (be sure to send a helper with them). Encourage everyone to handle the little creatures gently so they can be released, alive, after the safari.

Animal ABC
What you'll need: Circle of chairs

Children should be seated in a circle. The first youngster will name an animal that starts with A, the next one B, and so on through the alphabet. Be prepared to give a clue for each letter, if necessary, such as "It eats bananas" (monkey). If you feel that a letter is too hard, such as I, N, Q, U, V, and X, omit that one and go on to the next.

Animal Habits
What you'll need: Paper and envelopes

Prepare clues ahead of time by writing down the names of animals and placing the slips of paper in separate envelopes, one for each student.

At the safari, call the youngsters to the front of the group one at a time to take an envelope and pantomime the actions of the animal.

Allow three guesses from the rest of the group, asking them to raise hands and wait to be called on. Award fifteen points to the student who guesses correctly on the first try, ten points to the person who guesses correctly on the second attempt, and five points if it takes a third guess. If no one can get it after three attempts, the person pantomiming the animal announces what he is and receives fifteen points. A helper should keep track of the scores. At the end of the game, total the points and award a small stuffed animal or novelty toy to the winner.

REFRESHMENTS

Make or purchase a cake in the shape of a wild animal and add "jungle grass" to fit in with the theme. Color shredded coconut green by placing it in a jar and sprinkling in a few drops of food coloring. Shake vigorously until the coconut is coated, then spread it on a paper towel to dry. Sprinkle around the base of the cake.

DEVOTIONS

Focus your devotional on the awesome wonder of God's power in creation and His care. Have the children take turns reading verses 1, 10-12, 16-21, and 24-28 from Psalm 104, often called the Creation Psalm.

Direct the boys and girls to think about the animals mentioned in the Scripture passage. Ask, **Doesn't it amaze you that God thought to create all of them? What is more, He knows what each of them need in order to live. He gives them water to quench their thirst and food for their survival.**

Emphasize to the students that, as much as God cares for the animals, He cares for us even more. Read Matthew 6:25-26, then say the memory verse together. Close with prayer, thanking God for taking care of us.

INVITATION